Off to War

Franklin Countians in World War II

by Roscoe Barnes III

Burd Street Press

This Burd Street Press publication was printed by
Beidel Printing House, Inc.
63 West Burd Street
Shippensburg, PA 17257

In respect for the scholarship contained herein, the acid-free paper used in this book meets the guidelines for permanence and durability of the Committee on Production Guidelines for Book Longevity of the Council on Library Resources.

For a complete list of available publications please write:
Burd Street Press
Division of White Mane Publishing Company, Inc.
P.O. Box 152
Shippensburg, PA 17257

Dedication

This book is dedicated to Norman B. Rohrer, Sue Ernde, the memories of Ernie Pyle and all United States veterans of all times.

We have to remember that in the future we will want to keep before our children what this war was really like. It is so easy to forget; and then, for the younger generation, the heroism and the glamour remain, while the dirt, the hardships, the horror of death and the sorrow fade somewhat from their consciousness.

Eleanor Roosevelt

I wrote that I hoped the end of the war could be a gigantic relief, but not an elation. In the joyousness of high spirits it is easy for us to forget the dead. Those who are gone would not wish themselves to be a millstone of gloom around our necks. But there are many of the living who have had burned into their brains forever the unnatural sight of cold dead men scattered over the hillsides and in the ditches along the high rows of hedge throughout the world.

Ernie Pyle

Table of Contents

Part 4:
HOPING AGAINST HOPE
Keeping Faith as a Prisoner of War

Part 5:
CLOSE CALLS
A Combat Engineer Discovers the Power of Prayer

Part 6:
FINAL MOMENTS
The Bombing of Japan

Foreword

The Civil War historian's fervent dream is to interview a veteran who stood at Manassas with Jackson "like a stonewall," or advanced with the Virginians during Pickett's Charge, or who came to attention with Maj. Gen. Joshua Chamberlain and watched as the Confederate army's battered remnants laid down their arms and precious flags for the last time. Sadly, it is never to be; the last Civil War veteran died decades ago. We are all, as a nation, poorer for no longer being able to hear these men speak of their role in the war in which Americans were once enemies.

Unbeknownst to those who fought in the Civil War, that war was the great moral conflict of the twentieth century, and it too was a war to save humans from enslavement. Only a few decades from now historians will bemoan the fact that they did not have a chance to interview the World War II veterans before the last died out.

Roscoe Barnes III has written the book I wish I could have written. He has not only recorded these World War II veterans' statements about their roles in the most horrific war ever fought, but he has had the honor to sit face-to-face with the men who—though they deny it—are indeed great American heroes. Roscoe Barnes has thus given a gift to historians not yet born who will dream of talking to a veteran who ducked the burning gasoline from an exploding kamikaze, or who shivered in the cold horror of the Ardennes during the Battle of the Bulge, or who bled into the black volcanic sand of an island called Iwo Jima.

This book was written about the last generation, for the next, and for the many generations to come after. It is a literary time capsule about World War II and the common man and woman who fought it.

Mark Nesbitt, Author
Ghosts of Gettysburg series
35 Days to Gettysburg
Rebel Rivers
Saber and Scapegoats

PREFACE

"OKAY-LET'S GO"

With these words, Supreme Allied Commander Dwight D. Eisenhower, later to become President of the United States and to live in nearby Gettysburg, Pennsylvania, launched the Allied Invasion of Normandy which would eventually lead to the Allies' victory in Europe, thus ending the nightmare of Adolf Hitler and Nazi Germany which caused over 40 million deaths and casualties.

Three years before, all was quiet in the small communities of rural south central Pennsylvania, especially in Franklin County.

Charles McCleary, of Waynesboro, was in his junior year of high school. Though he had an upcoming math test, he was more occupied thinking about a special date he had on Saturday night. Little did he realize that, ten months later, he would be on a destroyer fighting Hitler's Germany and, on the same ship, participate in the Normandy Invasion and in the Invasion of Okinawa in 1945.

In November 1941, eighteen-year-old James Hammond of Fayetteville was just beginning to enjoy the opportunities and freedom life had to offer. Six months later, Jimi lost his freedom and began a nightmare of living Hell as a prisoner of war, being held captive by the Japanese for the next three years and three months.

Actions taken by individuals thousands of miles away in Berlin, Rome and Tokyo caused decisions to be made by individuals in London, Melbourne, Moscow and Washington, D.C., which altered the lives of these men and 10 million other men throughout America, forever.

From the farms, the classrooms, the shops and foundries, men throughout Franklin County were called upon to liberate continents, to bring freedom to enslaved millions, to bring an end to the horrors and destruction of WWII, and to change the face of the world. Many came home, returning to school, to jobs, returning to their wives and sweethearts, while others returned with wives, not returning to what was, but to forge and build anew. Those who didn't return gave up their tomorrows, assuring that those who did return would see and live tomorrow.

A tomorrow that would virtually wipe out a disease called Polio. A tomorrow that would see man walk on the moon. And a tomorrow that, unfortunately, would build a wall in Berlin that would serve as a symbol of an idea that enslaved 270 million men, women and children.

We've seen 300,000 Chinese, along with a replica of Lady Liberty, demonstrating for freedom in Tiennamen Square. We've seen the destruction of the Berlin Wall, not by guns, tanks or missiles, but by an idea. The same idea cherished by "GI JOE" as he crouched in his foxhole in Sicily. An idea the "Yank" died for at Kasserine Pass. An idea, first and foremost, symbolized in the raising of the American flag on Mt. Suribachi, an idea called freedom!

To the brave young men of Franklin County and their comrades, we give thanks. In place of memorials and monuments, their stories and fears, their laughter and tears shall serve as constant reminders etched in our hearts and lasting in our minds; of the enormous sacrifices and contributions these men made yesterday, so that we may live in freedom today and experience the joys of tomorrow.

For this is their story, as told by themselves, and it is through their actions that we salute the unsinkable American spirit! We lift our eyes to our flag and in so doing, we give thanks—thanks to God and to these brave men—and are proud to be Americans.

State Senator Terry Punt, R-33
Chairman Senate Military & Veteran Affairs Committee

Introduction

When Roscoe Barnes III joined *The Record Herald's* news staff in December 1994, one of his first assignments was a feature story about Bill Shoemaker.

The World War II veteran recounted his horrific experiences at the Battle of the Bulge 50 years before—in December, 1944.

Roscoe's story touched a nerve. Soon, World War II veterans were calling him weekly—many offering to tell their stories for the very first time.

Some of their wives sat in on the interviews. More than one wife told Roscoe afterwards: "That's the first time I've ever heard my husband talk about his war experiences."

One of Roscoe's many strengths is his ability to make people feel at ease, so I understand why those veterans were so willing to open up and share painful memories with him. Roscoe is a veteran himself, and I suspect that also inspired confidence in the men he interviewed.

What started with one interview grew into a series that ran in *The Record Herald* throughout most of 1995, fittingly the anniversary of the end of World War II.

Readers should keep in mind that Roscoe had many other tasks to do during that time—covering borough government and breaking news stories, writing obituaries, doing day-to-day police news—but he always found time for the World War II veterans, many times sacrificing his personal time and putting in long hours in the office.

Because of his willingness to "go the extra mile," future generations now will know of the sacrifices made by World War II veterans to end the scourge that was overtaking much of the world. Even after they are gone, their words and their thoughts will be forever preserved.

In 23 years in the newspaper business, I have read thousands of feature stories, but few have made me cry.

Several of Roscoe's stories did make me cry. Perhaps they will touch you as they touched me.

Sue Ernde
Editor
The Record Herald
Waynesboro, Pa.

PART 1

FAITH ON EUROPEAN SOIL
The Battles in Germany

William S. Shoemaker during the war.

1

William S. Shoemaker

WAYNESBORO—A shaken but determined teen-ager stood in silence as he peered across the frozen horizon. Men caught off guard became frightened. Some scurried for shelter. Most retreated and prayed for help.

The snow-covered grounds became an alley of horror, as death permeated the air. Bombs fell. Bullets flew. Pain erupted like a vicious volcano. The Battle of the Bulge had begun.

The year was 1944. The teen-ager was William S. Shoemaker of 220 Dickinson Avenue. He is 70 today, but as a 19-year-old, he served his country in World War II.

Although cold, exhausted and battle-worn, he drew on the strength of his faith and that of his comrades to rise to the occasion.

Shoemaker fought with the 30th Infantry Division, also known as the "work-horse of the Western Front."

He and his unit had been in Auchen when the Germans launched an attack in the Ardennes Forest in Belgium and Luxemburg.

"It was a surprise attack," said a calm and articulate Shoemaker. "They moved their troops in at night. They even disguised themselves by wearing American uniforms."

Shoemaker said he will never forget his first day in the Bulge.

"We were well spread out," he said, leaning forward. "I saw snow about four feet deep. I had no overcoat or galoshes. We were freezing!"

Sitting back, with his hands resting on the arms of his chair, Shoemaker recalled his terror.

"I looked down from the mountain and saw our people retreating."

He sits up.

"They had completely overran us!" he said of the Germans. "The only thing that was on my mind was praying to God that I would get out of there safely."

Shoemaker said he would be the first to admit his fear.

"I'm not afraid to say I was scared. If you're not scared in something like that, something is wrong with you."

Historians say the German attack on December 16, 1944, came as a total surprise to American forces. Even though Germany's generals knew they were beaten, the attack came as Adolf Hitler's final gamble.

Within two days, the Germans had advanced 15 miles and created a bulge in American (and Allied) lines 65 miles deep and 45 miles wide. Thus, it was called the Battle of the Bulge.

It was not until January, however, that the Germans were forced back to where they had been before the Bulge campaign. After the war, German documents revealed that in the Battle of the Bulge, the Germans came to respect American fighting abilities.

As the campaign was winding down, Shoemaker was wounded. On January 13, 1945, a mortar shell struck his left leg near the ankle.

Because it happened on his wife Leatrice's birthday, Shoemaker said he would never forget it. Also, he added, that day was his last on the front line.

He received a Purple Heart for his injury and a presidential citation for his service.

Shoemaker and his wife have been married since 1946. They have two sons and a daughter.

"I don't brag about my time in the war," he said, "I'm just proud of having served."

William S. Shoemaker holds the medal he received for an injury in the Battle of the Bulge.

Friends Forever

In addition to the support that his wife has given in his life, Shoemaker attributes much of his strength to his comrades in arms. The friends he served with during the war. They are the men of the 30th Infantry Division.

Each year, Shoemaker and the remaining few from his unit gather at each other's homes for a reunion where they share each other's memories—and undying friendship. Proudly they acknowledge being friends forever.

On May 20, 1995, nine of those men gathered at Shoemaker's home, where they laughed, they joked and exchanged stories.

"Some of the stories are the same," said Shoemaker, "but we never get tired of hearing them. It helps us to talk about these things."

Under a beaming sun and the shade of a pup tent, the men and their wives mingled with food and lots of fun. They also took time from their fun to remember the dead.

In a moving prayer that brought quite a few tears, veteran Junious Bost of Kannapolis, North Carolina, asked for blessings over the meal and for God's help in filling the void left by the deceased.

During the reunion, the men reviewed maps, books and various relics of years gone by.

The reunion started in the late 1970s at the urging of Bost's wife. He had been sending Christmas cards to Harlan "Red" Eastlick of Montana.

"We hadn't seen each other for 33 years," Bost said. "Then my wife said: 'You have been talking about this man for many years, why not call him?' "

Bost called him and arranged for a get-together.

Shortly after they met, the men decided to locate the other men in their regiment. They began their search with a map that had been signed by the men during the war. Luckily, they were able to find 15 of the 44 people in their platoon.

"Fifteen showed up at my house," said Bost. From there, they started meeting every two years.

In the mid-1980s, Shoemaker took note of the ages of his World War II buddies and decided they should meet at least once a year. They've been meeting annually since 1988.

"These meetings show what we're made of," said one vet. "After all these years, we still get together."

Ardie Winters during the war.

2

ARDIE WINTERS

WAYNESBORO—Two skeletal men rushed out from the building when they heard the Americans coming.

The men were haggard. Their eyes were sunken. They could barely stand. They were dying of starvation.

One man found flour and buried his face in it. He started heaving as the flour covered his grimy beard. His bony limbs, like twigs on a dying tree, began to shake as he forced the powder down his throat.

The other snatched a beef shin bone and started gnawing.

"They were so glad to see us," recalls Ardie Winters, who witnessed that scene in Germany in 1945, as World War II was winding down. "We had to stop the first man to keep him from hurting himself. Those guys hadn't eaten for months."

Winters, in his mid-20s at the time, was a staff sergeant in the 3rd Army Division, 99th Infantry.

He and his men were moving south of Kassel when they stumbled on the prisoner-of-war camp, where about 200 Russians were imprisoned.

"They were so thin," Winters said, noting he'd never seen a man so small. "They had long dirty hair and long beards. You could see their bones. What little clothes they had were barely hanging on them."

Exploding Bodies

Winters saw a lot during the war. Like other soldiers, he saw things that could make a brave man shudder...things that would melt even the coldest heart.

Yet, what he saw in Brest, France, would change him forever.

"It was there that my hair turned gray," he recalls.

The Germans used Brest as an underground submarine base. But before approaching the base, Winters and his men stayed in a wooded area for 17 days.

"We laid outside there not knowing what was going on. We were in foxholes," he recalls. "It was in September, and it was hot.

"All around were dead animals—cows and everything. Some had been dead for weeks. And because of the heat, their bodies started to swell and explode. They were exploding all around us."

And if that wasn't bad enough, when Winters' crew hit the base, they found it empty—of living soldiers. The bodies of enemy soldiers were buried only a few inches under ground.

Like the animals' corpses, they, too, were swollen and started exploding because of the heat. The odor was unbearable.

"I didn't eat for three days," Winters recalls. "I tell you, it's one thing to smell animal bodies. But human bodies? After they've been out there for three weeks? That's an awful smell."

Winters' men moved about the area squinting and pressing handkerchiefs against their noses. Some threw up. Some staggered from dizziness.

Others, however, moved farther into the base and found cases of good wine.

"I guess there were officers' quarters there. I couldn't eat, but we drank some and buried the rest of the wine in a crater," Winters said. "We never went back to get it."

"Ungodly Cold"

Following the invasion of France, Winters moved on to Germany, were he fought in the Battle of the Bulge. In addition to the blood, Winters remembers the cold.

Ardie Winters holds a photo of himself taken during World War II.

"It was so ungodly cold. We had to take off our shoes and massage our feet every hour."

Some of the men suffered frostbite and lost their feet. Then others, while removing their boots, found their skin coming off with their socks.

The men did not bathe for weeks at a time.

Following the Bulge, Winters and his men found themselves on the Rhine River, a major border line—and avenue of transportation in Europe.

The Allies had learned the Germans were blowing up bridges in an attempt to keep the Allies out of the country. Word soon spread that the Remagen Bridge also would be blown.

One morning, soon after the sun appeared, Winters and his crew mounted the bridge. He saw numerous bodies on the bridge, some of which were American soldiers.

Not knowing when the bridge would blow, Winters told his men to follow him, and they shot off across the bridge. Leaping over bodies, maneuvering through debris and machinery, he sprinted some 440 yards and was the first to reach the other side.

"I set a record that morning," he says. "We jumped over our own men who'd been killed. I never ran so fast in my life."

Before the war, Winters had been an athlete at Smithsburg High School, where he ran track and played basketball. At 6-1 and 165 pounds, he also was a high jumper.

Today, Winters lives with his wife, Charlotte, at 119 Garfield Street. Every once in a while, a friend will watch a movie about the Remagen Bridge and call Winters.

"Hey Ardie," he says. "I saw you running across the Remagen last night."

Winters laughs.

General Patton

Following the incident along the Rhine River, Winters had an opportunity to see the legendary General George S. Patton Jr., commander of the 3rd Army Division.

"He was rough," said Winters. "He was the 'old blood and guts' like they called him. He was firm. He told us: 'You can do it. We're gonna kill those d____ krauts!' "

Winters said Patton had broad shoulders but was not very tall.

"We never saw him smile," he said.

As the war was drawing down, Winters would have other moments he would call unforgettable. One such moment occurred south of Kassel, when a German tank fired on his crew and killed one of his gunmen.

"They took his head and shoulder right off. When that happened, I went around to the side of the tank and grabbed a bazooka."

Winters struck the tank from the side and destroyed it. He was awarded a Bronze Star for his actions.

Prayer

A soldier can learn a lot of things in war, according to Winters. That's especially true with religion, as with one soldier who wanted to pray.

"We were dug in off of the Rhine River," Winters said. "They were shelling us and we were out of rations. They kept throwing mortars at us."

Dug in shallow foxholes amid rocks and stones, a corporal crawled over.

"Sarge," he said. "How do you pray?"

The soldier was frightened.

"He was rough and tough," said Winters. "He wasn't too well educated."

Winters looked at him.

"He crawled over on his belly," Winters said. "I told him to just talk to God like you talk to me. Put the Lord's name in the place of mine and ask for his help."

"He did that and none of us were killed."

A Joyous Day

As the war was drawing to a close, Winters said few people can imagine what it was like for American soldiers, especially on V-J Day

Ardie Winters greets his wife, Charlotte, on his arrival at Fort Dix, N.J. in 1945.

(Victory over Japan). He was at home in Waynesboro when he learned that Japan had surrendered. He was discharged right before it happened.

"It was a joyous day," he said. "I didn't want to go back to Europe and I sure didn't want to go to Japan."

Winters, now a borough councilman, had returned home in June 1945 on a 45-day furlough. His wife was the first to greet him.

"I met my wife in Fort Dix, New Jersey," he said. "It was quite a thrill. I hadn't seen her in 3 1/2 years."

Besides his family, Winters said he also was happy to see his favorite dish: a strawberry shortcake. His mother-in-law served him an "oversized dish of it," and he ate it all in one sitting. Later, he would have stomach cramps as his body adjusted to sugar and hot meals.

"We were used to dry rations," he said. "My stomach had shrunk."

But where was he on V-J Day? And what was he doing? Winters and his dad were racing across lawns—and streets—to reach the downtown parade.

"My daddy fell and dropped his speed-graphic camera," he recalled, laughing. "He tripped over a curb, got up and kept running. We both made it to the parade."

After the celebration, Winters made a big adjustment when he re-entered the civilian work-force. He returned to his old job in retail management. But things were different.

"You could think again...for yourself. In the Army, you followed orders. I had to change my philosophy of dealing with people," he said.

Kenneth H. Hess during the war.

3

Kenneth H. Hess

WAYNESBORO—Kenneth H. Hess was taking a cigarette out of his friend's pocket when a shot rang out.

He turned and saw his friend falling: A sniper had shot him between the eyes.

"When he fell to the ground, he had a death grip on my jacket sleeve."

That's what Hess remembers about one of his many battles in World War II. He was in Sigolsheim, Germany, at the time.

"I believe the sniper meant to kill me," Hess said. "The same sniper had killed one of my men just a few minutes before that."

Hess, who lives at 11833 Country Club Road, has seen his share of blood and battles. Born July 10, 1924, he joined the U.S. Army in 1943 at the age of 18.

In addition to Germany, he served in France, Italy, North Africa and Austria. All together, he spent 320 days on the front lines, including 111 days in one area.

"I've walked all over Germany," he said. "I was tired."

Hess served in Company G, 2nd Battalion, 15th Infantry Regiment in the 3rd Infantry Division. Despite his age, he achieved the rank of first sergeant in less than three years.

For the last 17 years, the 70-year-old Hess has battled Parkinson's disease. He recently had his second bypass surgery. He moves with a cane.

Before his retirement, he owned and operated Hess Custom Builders, now run by his two sons.

Despite his physical limitations, his mind remains sharp. Easily, he can recall names, locations and dates, including date of action and the dates on which his troops were wounded or killed in action.

A short time ago, Hess received a call from an Erie woman who was planning a trip to Europe. Because her father had been killed in the war, she wanted to know how and where it happened.

When Hess took the phone, he told her he remembered her father. After telling her where he died, she asked him how it happened.

"It was too horrible," Hess told her, declining to elaborate.

Yes, his mind is sharp. But that's not all. His countenance is strong. His character is polished. He bears the marks of one who has known courage, service and hard work.

Whether the person killed was a private or a captain, Hess can rattle off dates and times. He also remembers faces and conversations.

He said others have contacted him over the years with questions about the war. He rarely fails to help them, given his memory and the papers he has kept.

His Journal

One of the reasons Hess can recall the many events in the war is that he kept a journal containing detailed and meticulous notes.

For instance, in 1943, he wrote:

* Oct. 13— Co. crossed Volturno with heavy casualties. Water was waist deep. We dug in on the high hill north of the Volturno.

* Oct. 28—Attacked hill north of San Felice and fought all day and only had 4 EM (enlisted men) killed and 5 EM wounded and 1 officer wounded. We took our objective.

* Oct. 31—I made Pfc. at Pietravairono, Italy.

In 1944, he wrote:

* Dec. 25—Made 2 attacks on the hill on this Xmas Day and the krauts cut us off and captured about 60 of our men and countless numbers of our men were killed and wounded. Most of the men that

were wounded we couldn't get to, and they froze to death for it was zero weather at that time.

* Dec. 27—We finally took the hill with the help of a Sherman tank and we had to walk and step on the dead boys who had been killed before in the attacks that we made.

* Dec. 28—Attacked the town of Sigolsheim where I had 7 men killed and 6 seriously wounded.

Hess has taken great pains to preserve his journal, along with letters, notes and other papers from the war era. He keeps them neatly in a box. They are brown with age.

A Grandson's Report

Hess's journal has not only been helpful to him, but to others. Last year, his grandson, Clint E. Rock, used the journal to write a report for a class project.

"There are many...stories my grandfather could tell," he wrote.

"For good luck while in the Army, my grandfather Hess always carried a silver dollar strung around his neck on his dog tags and a Bible in his pocket. In the Bible, he carried a picture of his mother, Iva Hess.

"As I interviewed him, he took the silver dollar out of his desk drawer, turning the coin in the palm of his hand. He said, 'If this thing could talk, I could imagine the stories it could tell.'

"My grandfather Hess is a man who will be remembered for his faith and his courage," Clint wrote.

Audie Murphy

In addition to remembering friends and troops in his unit, Hess also recalls serving with the renowned Audie Murphy, the most decorated soldier in World War II.

"Yeah, I saw him," said Hess, who described him as a little guy who was always busy.

There was nothing unusual about Murphy, Hess noted. He looked like an average guy. "He had no idea he would receive those awards," Hess said.

Murphy received 24 medals from the U.S. government, three from the French and one from the Belgians. He later became an actor,

Kenneth H. Hess displays his jacket from the war era.

starring in such films as "The Red Badge of Courage" and "To Hell and Back."

When Hess saw Murphy, the soon-to-be star was helping a wounded soldier near a pill box in Germany.

"Audie, how are you?" Hess asked.

"All right, fellow, but I'm busy," Murphy replied.

Later, on the same day that Murphy received the Congressional Medal of Honor, Hess received the Silver Star.

The First to Die

Although Hess may have legitimate cause for boasting, that is something he will never do. In fact, when he speaks about the war, there is no delight.

When he refers to certain moments, he drops his head. Water wells up in his eyes. His wife, Jane, asks if he's okay.

The pain is real, the memories still vivid.

It all seems unbearable when he talks about Roy "Mooch" Mowen, the first Waynesboro man to die in World War II.

Mowen was on Mount Lungo in Italy, November 18,1943, when he was killed.

"There was nothing between us and the Germans but open ground," Hess said. "They started shelling in right over us.

"Mooch asked, 'What are we gonna do now?'

" 'Just follow me,' I told him."

They ran with all the speed they could muster.

Then Mooch said, "Kenny, I believe I'm hit."

"Where?" asked Hess.

He placed a hand on Mooch and felt for the wound.

"I felt nothin' but blood. It was real sticky," Hess said.

Mooch asked for a drink of water.

"We don't have any," Hess said, then tried to administer first aid.

"Kenny, I got some cigarettes there in my pocket," Mooch said. "You can have them."

They were Lucky Strikes in a green package.

Those were the last words that Hess would hear from Mooch.

Richard W. McFadden during the war.

4

Richard W. McFadden

FORT LOUDON—Richard W. McFadden was a star athlete who shined brightly. But, like a falling star, his burst of light was soon dimmed—and his future cut short—when he was killed in Germany during World War II.

Today, his name is still remembered in Fort Loudon, the place where he grew up. It evokes pictures of his daring feats on the baseball field, his dashing speed on the track and his breath-taking jumps.

He was considered the greatest all-around athlete of Franklin County, according to officials of the South Central Chapter of the Pennsylvania Sports Hall of Fame.

On November 1, 1990, they inducted him into the South Central Chapter Pennsylvania Sports Hall of Fame.

"His natural physical talents were balanced with a desire to excel, and it showed in basketball, baseball, track and soccer," they said.

McFadden was born on November 13, 1923. He was the son of Calvin and Goldie Brandt McFadden.

His brother, Ronald, remembers his youthful vigor.

"He was pretty big. He stood about 6-3 and weighed 195 pounds," he said. "He never smoked or drank. He just loved to play ball."

"Oh, he was very muscular," said his sister, Helen Pensinger. "He had a wonderful personality!"

According to *The Fort Loudon News* (October 5, 1990), former teacher and coach, Howard M. Hege of Chambersburg, knew Richard from 1934 to 1941.

Won Every Game

Hege taught two grades and was coach of the teams. With Richard playing, Fort Loudon Elementary School won every game, he remembered.

Later, Hege transferred to Lemasters High School (now James Buchanan) and continued to coach teams in soccer, baseball, basketball and track. While there, McFadden came aboard. While he was on the team, Lemasters had a 15-4 season and the next year a 16-3 season.

They were county champions and ended up second in the state in District III, Class B.

"Dick played centerfield on the baseball team, but could he hit!" Hege said.

Richard also was remembered as a one-man track team. Lemasters had no track, according to *The Fort Loudon News*, but McFadden entered the county, district and state meets.

"He was the team. Track proved what a terrific athlete he was," said Hege.

After Richard entered three events at the state meet at State College, he took two first places (shot-put and discus) and a second place, receiving 14 points.

"These points gave Lemasters High School a tie for fifth place in the state," said Hege. "These records still stand."

"Dick was the best athlete that I ever coached," Hege said. "I coached track at Chambersburg High School from 1948 to 1955 and had some good boys, but Dick was the best."

Dr. Luther Lausch of Reading, Pennsylvania, agreed with Hege. He said McFadden had the potential to become a college star and a major league player in any of several sports.

"Not only was he a super athlete, but he was as fine a young man as anyone could ever hope to coach," he said.

Helen Pensinger and Ronald McFadden.

New York Yankees

Ronald said his brother was good in everything he attempted, but he especially loved baseball.

"I'm telling you, he loved baseball. He ate it and slept it. He could hit a ball a country mile. I'm sure he'd been up there with Babe Ruth."

He said his brother, while a teenager, developed a reputation for breaking windows and hitting balls over the fence.

"My dad took him out to the Harrisburg Senators. They wanted to see him. He hit everything," Ronald said. "So they brought out their best pitchers. He kept hitting them."

Later, McFadden was electrifying crowds at Henniger Field in Chambersburg when he caught the eye of a New York Yankee scout.

"The scout didn't know him or my Dad," said Ronald. "My dad heard him say: 'Who's that guy hitting them over the fence?'"

"'That's my son,' my Daddy said."

Richard was later offered a contract by the Yankees.

On another occasion, a man came to Richard's house to inquire about some broken windows. He had owned a plant and during baseball, McFadden would break out several windows because of hitting the ball out of the park.

"Who's breaking my windows?" the man asked Richard's dad.

"My son is. I owe you anything?"

"Naw," said the man. "Here's some ice cream."

Mercersburg Academy

Although Richard was tempted to take the many offers thrown his way, his dad, said Ronald, wanted him to get a good education.

"Back in those days, we didn't have TV. Everybody had a good team. But Dad wanted him to get a good education," he said.

Richard was encouraged to attend Mercersburg Academy.

He went there from 1941 to 1942 where he won the Williams Cup. In a school renowned for its track teams, Richard captured the cup which was presented each year to the athlete who scores the highest number of points in special competition that included six events: 120 low hurdles, the 100-yard dash, the high jump, long jump, shot-put and javelin.

"Richard won all six events," said Helen, his sister. "He was the first to do so since the cup's inception in 1903."

Reportedly, several previous winners left Mercersburg to go gain Olympic fame.

After Richard's big win one day, Helen said members of the McConnellsburg baseball team were disgruntled. Their team had been trounced by Fort Loudon.

She was out minding the gas pump in Fort Loudon when the members stopped by.

"McFadden. McFadden. That's all we heard," a member said.

"Be careful," responded Helen. "I'm a McFadden."

The War

Richard was drafted into the U.S. Army in June 1943. He served in the 29th Infantry Division.

"They put him with a mechanized reconnaissance outfit because he was a runner," Helen said, adding his only hope was to one day return home and play baseball. He also wanted to marry.

Pensinger remembers stories she heard about her brother during the war: One time, a German stole his jeep. Richard ran after him, and the German was surprised to step out of the jeep to find Richard right on him.

"(Richard) stepped smartly into the jeep, wheeled it around and sped down the road before the German could think to fire," she said in *The Fort Loudon News*.

Another time, when he was attacked by the Germans, he leaped over a hedgerow and escaped. He went back later and measured the hedgerow that proved to be seven feet high.

He wrote: "You can do anything with bullets up your back."

Helen said Richard shared these experiences with her husband, Lloyd Pensinger. Richard "used to tell him things rather than tell his mother because he didn't want her to worry."

Despite his many talents—and his love for sports—Richard's dream of being a professional player would not materialize.

On November 26, 1944, Richard was killed at Alsdorf, Germany, near the breakthrough in the Battle of the Bulge.

Like many promising athletes during his era, his talents died with him.

"We couldn't believe he was killed," said Ronald, recalling a letter from his brother.

In the letter, dated October 1944—weeks before his death—Richard expressed his longing love for baseball.

"I sure would like to have a chance to play some baseball," he wrote, "but I don't know where or when I'd ever get the chance."

Robert W. Florence during the war.

5

ROBERT W. FLORENCE

WAYNESBORO—There is a reason why many World War II veterans do not talk about the war, according to Robert W. Florence.

"I've never talked about my experiences. The subject is hard to talk about. Why? Because we had to kill human beings and destroy their homes. It was them, or us," said Florence who served with the 303rd Engineer Battalion from 1941 to 1946.

Florence, who lives with his wife Betty at 349 West Eighth Street, enlisted in the Army at age 20.

"I enlisted in 1941," he said. "Everybody said if you get in now, you'll have a better chance at getting a promotion and commission."

Florence found himself training as a combat engineer. Unlike civilian engineers, those in the military did not spend time reading blue prints and constructing nice buildings, Florence said. They instead focused on building bridges and blowing them up.

"It was about demolition, as well as construction," Florence said.

NO POWER TOOLS

During the war, his unit traveled throughout various places in Germany. Braving the freezing elements of winter, Florence and his

Robert W. Florence in 1995.

men relied on sweat, determination and ingenuity under pressure to build what was needed to move American troops.

"In those days, we had no power tools," he said. "We did everything by hand, using pick-shovels and hammers."

The corps of engineers often tore up railroad tracks and cut down trees, and used anything they could to build a bridge.

"We had some boys from Maine who were lumberjacks. They were good," Florence said.

German Civilians

Although Florence can now talk about the war, the words come as a struggle. He speaks slowly as if reluctant to discuss what may be forbidden.

He frowns when he speaks about the Remagen Bridge in Germany.

"When we crossed the Rhine River, there were exclusive homes. Our boys smashed everything," he said. "The German women were crying."

In broken English, they cried, "Don't do this!"

In some places, the women and other German civilians were given weapons, Florence said. But they were given in vain. The reason is that a good many Germans "were happy to see us." Florence said most relinquished their weapons and showed a sign of relief when they saw American soldiers.

As for destroying their homes, Florence said he felt bad about it. His troops had been ordered to respect the homes of civilians.

"We gave orders to 'remember you're civilized.' But when your buddies lie beside you bleeding to death and people are shooting at you, things happen. That's war."

No matter how much respect one may have for property, Florence said something happens to a man who sees blood each day for years at a time, especially when the bleeding is caused by the enemy. Some simply break and explode under the pressure, he said.

Incidentally, Florence saw one thing that left him puzzled. Something small but appealing. As an engineer, he could not—and still can't—understand how the Germans kept fresh eggs.

"They had eggs in a water bottle. They were preserved... fresh, like they'd just come out of a chicken. I still don't know how they kept those eggs.

"Still, we ate a lot of them."

Prisoners of War

The sight that shook many Americans was the condition of the Poles and Jews in Prisoner of War (POW) camps, Florence said. He and his men found such camps in 1944 and 1945.

"You just couldn't believe it," he said with a look of anger and bewilderment. "How in the hell can men do something like this to other human beings?"

Florence took pictures of the starving men. He has them today.

In a dark and eerie scene, the men, mostly Jews, are piled on top of each other. Most are naked. Their bones are prominent. Their faces bear a ghostly stare. They were all dying.

"No one can tell me this didn't happen," Florence said. "I saw it with my own eyes—and so did my men."

For the Poles, Florence's men put TNT in a stream to blow up fish. The freed Poles ate the fish as fast as they could. For the Jews, it was different.

"They were treated the worst," Florence said. "They were in no condition to do anything."

Florence shakes his head. His eyes water.

"You can't imagine what it was like," he said.

"Colored Soldiers"

In addition to blood, German civilians and POW camps, Florence also remembers when black soldiers became a part of his unit.

"There were no blacks in combat at that time," he said. "It was close to the end. They sent some colored men. Each battalion took them and used them for combat."

Florence said it was strange, at first, for some of his men. "For some of them, it was their first time being with colored men. But not me, I've known them most of my life," he said.

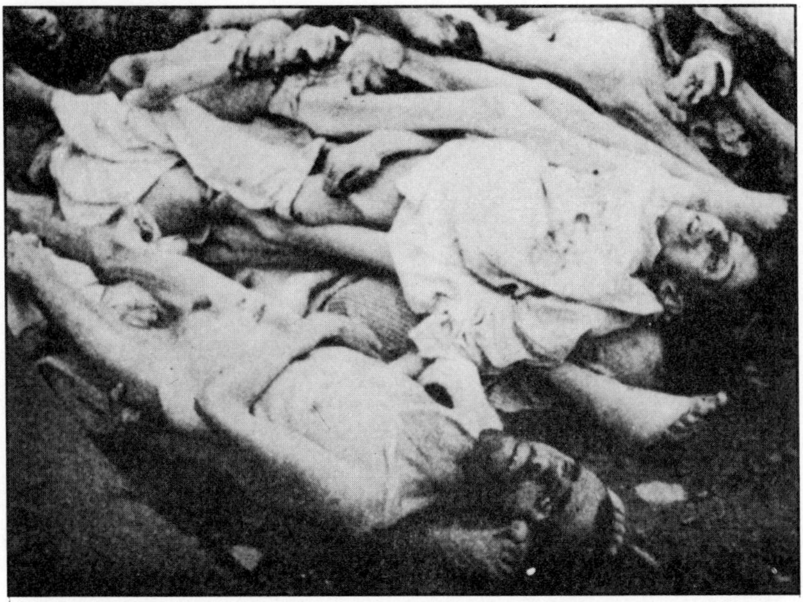

Photos of Concentration Camps taken by Robert W. Florence.

The colonel used the black soldiers for "fire power to help cover our men while they moved forward," Florence said, adding they put on an impressive show of gallantry.

"My colonel said, 'If I ever need fire power, I want these men with me,' " Florence said.

Victory Over Japan

Toward the end of the war, Florence was still in Germany. In fact, when Japan surrendered in August 1945, Florence was erecting a fence for a POW camp in Germany.

"When we heard the news, we sent a truck into the French zone. It came back with 110 gallons of wine," he said.

The Americans and German prisoners all drank wine together and celebrated the end of the war.

"That day, everybody loved everybody," Florence said. "I don't regret a day of what I had to do."

PART 2

THEY SAW THE FLAG

The Fight for Iwo Jima

Bill Adams poses on March 9, 1945 with his ship's mascot, Cocoa, which was picked up in Cuba.

6

Bill Adams

WAYNESBORO—Although Bill Adams is modest about his experiences at Iwo Jima during World War II, he has a profound respect for the U.S. Marines who served with him.

"Since then, and for the rest of my life, I'll have respect for them," he said.

Adams remembers taking casualties off the beach when someone told them a flag was going up.

"We knew it was symbolic, but we had no idea what it would come to mean."

The U.S. Marines raised the American flag on Mount Suribachi on February 23, 1945, during what is considered one of the bloodiest campaigns of World War II. A photo taken of the same has come to symbolize American patriotism and heroism during the war.

"I saw the flag," said Adams, who was 18 at the time.

"We knew the Marines had secured the ground. They took the ground, but they would face four more weeks of terrible fighting to secure the northern end of the island."

About 25,000 Marines were killed or wounded on Iwo Jima.

The Beginning

Adams, 68, who lives with his wife, Joanne, at 80 East Second Street, would go on to serve 27 years in the military. He retired in 1970 from the U.S. Army National Guard.

The Adamses are the proud parents of five children.

Although 50 years have passed since Adams walked the shores of Iwo Jima, located about 750 miles south of Japan, he vividly recalls the blood, the fear and the thundering sounds of battle.

Adams served as a Fireman First Class in the U.S. Navy. He enlisted on January 19, 1944, only days after his 18th birthday. The next month, he was assigned to the LST390 ship, where he learned he would go to Iwo Jima.

"When we were told, it didn't mean that much to us. You know, we were young. We knew only of the location, that it was close to Japan," he said.

The Island

The island, 8 miles square with a landscape of volcanic rubble, was occupied by 21,000 Japanese soldiers. The Japanese were using Iwo Jima as a fighter airbase and well-fortified fighting ground.

The Americans wanted to use the island as another base from which to step up their bombing campaign against Japan. When they arrived, they found the Japanese "dug in" through a system of caves and tunnels.

"We got there late in the evening on February 18th," Adams recalls. "It was cold and damp, especially that night. We could see old battle ships, and we could tell they had been bombing the island for quite a while."

Adams said nobody slept that night.

"You couldn't do much sleeping or anything. We just made ready for the next day."

The next morning, Adams' ship unloaded about 130 soldiers.

And there it happened.

Bill Adams holds up a picture of his crew, taken during the war.

Historians say the conquest of the island proved the hardest fight the Marines faced in the Pacific. From the moment they went ashore, they were under continuous heavy bombardment from well-hidden gun positions.

Violent Deaths

The Marines, crowded on the beaches, found no shelter from the shellfire.

According to Robert Sherrod, journalist: "They died with the greatest possible violence. Nowhere in the Pacific have I seen such badly mangled bodies. Many were cut squarely in half. Legs and arms lay 50 feet away from any body."

Adams saw it all.

He did not engage in battle like the Marines, but he assisted, relentlessly, with the wounded and others. Adams said he left the island the same day the flag went up.

The flag, he said, will always remain in his memory.

Today, the raising of the flag is a model for the Marine Corps monument in Arlington Cemetery in Washington, D.C.

"I don't feel like I did very much, but the Marines? I'll always respect them."

Eugene Monn at home in 1945.

7

EUGENE MONN

ROUZERVILLE—Fifty years ago, Eugene Monn stood nervously aboard a ship in troubled waters. From there he saw a battered island become a blazing inferno.

There he heard shelling, bombing and the cries of dying men. The stench of burning flesh and dead bodies burned in his nostrils. A cloud of smoke—and the sizzling rounds of diehard Japanese—affected his vision.

Yet, on February 23, 1945, Monn saw a ray of hope—that inch of a chance that he would live and return home. That day, from the shores of Iwo Jima, he saw his fellow Marines raise the American flag on the top of Mount Suribachi.

"They raised the flag right before we went ashore," said Monn, who was 22 at the time.

"I saw it from the ship. We were all happy. We said, 'Ah Boy, this is almost over!' "

That elation, however, was short lived. For as Monn, a Marine with the 3rd Marine Division, was approaching the shores of Iwo Jimo, he suddenly realized the battle was not over.

"We had no idea what we were getting into. The Japanese were shelling the heck out of us," he said.

Four more weeks would follow on the island in what would be the bloodiest battle ever for the U.S. Marines in the Pacific Islands.

Today, Monn, of 11466 Buchanan Trail East, is 72. He lives with his wife Grace, whom he married October 30, 1948. They have one son, Todd.

Despite Monn's age, he maintains the looks of a hardcore Marine. His spirit is strong. His movements, quick.

"Once a Marine, always a Marine," his wife chuckles.

What He Saw

Sitting in his living room, leaning forward, he rests his elbows on top of his knees.

"I wouldn't take a million dollars for what I've seen and done," he says. "But I wouldn't take a dollar to do it again."

Monn says he doesn't like to talk about his experiences during the war. Although he hasn't had nightmares, he said he thinks about it all the time, especially when someone mentions it.

He says he's seen too much blood. Too much dying.

"The worst thing I saw was the piles of dead bodies of dead soldiers, not just the Marines.

"Those sights you never forget."

While on the island, just 750 miles south of Japan, Monn spent more than a month in a foxhole. He also worked as sergeant in intelligence.

Monn, who joined the Corps in September 1942, said he is proud to have served his country. He said he'll always appreciate the discipline he received.

Coming Home

When Monn looks back, he remembers his father.

"When I left for the war, my father's hair was black. When I returned, his hair was as white as a shirt," he said. "He had four sons overseas at one time."

Monn returned to the States in May 1945. In August, when Japan surrendered, he was assigned to the Philadelphia Navy Yard.

Eugene Monn holds a quadrant, a measuring device the Japanese used when firing their weapons on Iwo Jima.

"My uncle and I were in a bar," he recalled. "We heard sirens go off and a lot of noise when the news came down. The bartender then locked the door and said my uncle and I could stay."

Monn said the news was a sigh of relief, as he had been scheduled to "go back overseas again."

Coming home was a great experience for Monn. He arrived in Waynesboro on September 26, 1945. Everything was different, he said, except the food he loved.

"The thing I missed a lot was good ole home cooking," he said with a big grin. "My mother was the best cook."

After being reacquainted with family members and friends, Monn got a job with a lumber company. He started out as a truck driver and was promoted to yard foreman. Later, he became a salesman and store manager, before retiring.

Because of his experiences in the war, he said he has learned to get along with anybody.

"It taught you that, and to appreciate life," he said.

PART 3

AMID WAVES OF TERROR

Battles in the Water

Charles McCleary during the war.

8

Charles McCleary

WAYNESBORO—It was near midnight when Charles McCleary said he would go up to get a helmet. For hours, he and others aboard the USS *Shubrick* had heard a lot of planes and gunfire.

They were en route to a radar picket station 50 miles west of Okinawa, when two enemy aircrafts attacked. They fired and shot down the first plane.

The second one, however, made a dead hit.

It was 12:13 a.m., May 29, 1945, when the Japanese suicide plane crashed into the *Shubrick.* Twenty men were killed, 25 wounded and 15 missing in action.

McCleary scrambled to save the ship and to assist the other men.

"We hurried to put out the main fire. But there were spot fires all around," he recalls.

Non-sentimental

Those experiences 50 years ago remain fresh in McCleary's memory. Yet, he is not morbid or overly sentimental when he talks about them. He simply acknowledges the horror and the fear he felt.

Recently, McCleary visited Washington, D.C. to talk about his experiences. He participated in an "Invasion of Okinawa" ceremony and was interviewed by CNN, CBS and the *Washington Times.*

Today, McCleary is 70. He retired in 1986 as Waynesboro's chief of police. He lives with his wife, Rebecca, on Green Street. They have four daughters.

McCleary was 17 when he joined the U.S. Navy in 1942. He was 20 when his ship was hit.

He had participated in three invasions: Sicily, D-Day Normandy and Southern France.

The Diary

During the Okinawa invasion, his friend kept a diary. He wrote: "The plane dropped a bomb just an instant before she crashed. The bomb hit the deck, spreading fire all over."

McCleary remembers walking out with a helmet when the plane hit his ship. The bomb, carried by the plane, exploded on the main deck.

"The plane hit and blew me back up the deck. My friend, Golden, got a hose and tried to put the fire out," he says.

Later, a depth charge, similar to a cannon, exploded and caused a great shock and concussion. The explosion blew the fire out, but not without doing further damage.

"It blew the fire out," said McCleary. "And Golden, it blew him apart. His head was blown off!"

Sadly enough, McCleary says he and the crew had kidded Golden about being killed.

"The Japs are going to get you," they would say, not really meaning it.

When Golden died, "we felt like hell," McCleary says. "But there's nothing you can do about it."

McCleary said despite the courage shown by American men, fear was like a stubborn shadow during the attacks: It would not leave.

"What You Had To Do..."

"You were scared stiff," he recalls, "but you did what you had to do."

Charles McCleary holds a flag which was burned in the attack on the USS *Shubrick*.

Looking back on his experiences, McCleary says he, like other veterans, learned some important things about life.

In a matter-of-fact tone, he says he has seen a lot of deaths, including those of his close friends.

"No, I have no regrets about serving in the war. I wouldn't have missed it for the world," he says. Still, it's not something he would want to do again.

"I'm just lucky to be alive."

Elwood B. Bumbaugh during the war.

9

Elwood B. Bumbaugh

ROUZERVILLE—When Elwood B. Bumbaugh came home in the fall of 1944, he was scared and restless.

At the age of 21, he had tasted combat. In a fierce battle aboard the USS *Franklin*, he had seen the terror of Japanese "Kamikazes" or suicide pilots. For six months in the Philippines, he fought in the greatest naval battle of all times, the Battle for Leyte Gulf.

But then on leave, he was worried, says his younger brother, Creston C. Bumbaugh of Rouzerville.

"He came home and said, 'If you know what's good for you, you'll stay out of there for as long as you can,' " Creston recalls.

A few months later, on March 19, 1945, Elwood died in battle. His ship, the USS *Franklin*, had suffered a fatal blow.

An Old Letter

Today, Creston still remembers his brother. He stood about 6 feet, with a strong but thin frame. His hair was black and his eyes, dark brown. He was full of life.

Sitting in his home at 12334 Old Pen Mar Road, Creston reaches for an envelope. It is brown and nearly brittle with age.

"Here's a letter from my brother," he says, lurching forward.

The letter is dated August 20, 1944. He opens the envelope in haste, seeming anxious—and proud.

"It feels a little strange," he says with a nervous grin. The memories are strong.

In the letter, Elwood asks about Creston's dating and the well-being of a nephew. He had written at other times, trying to mention the weather or his location and work, but those items commonly were deleted because of censorship during the war, Creston explained.

He reads the letter and pauses.

"Yeah, we were close. You think about it. We all worked at Pen Mar park when we were kids," he says.

Suicide Bombs

The two brothers did much together, despite the four-year age difference. They worked on the farm just off Old Pen Mar Road and played the guitar whenever they could. Country music was Elwood's favorite, and "Silver Hair Daddy" was his song of choice.

All that changed in the fall of 1944. Elwood had changed. He seemed different, says Creston. For death had become his prowler. He could sense its presence.

He had a feeling that something bad soon would happen—something worse than he had already seen.

"He was highly nervous. He could hardly sit still," says Creston, noting the battle for Leyte Gulf may have caused the change.

It was during that battle that Americans were introduced to "Kamikazes." The word actually meant "divine wind." It referred to the vicious typhoon which destroyed a Chinese invasion fleet in the 13th century as it headed toward Japan.

The kamikaze pilots of World War II flew in old airplanes loaded with explosives. Whenever they found the American fleet, the pilots tried to crash their planes into American ships. They hoped their own death would cause the enemy to lose a vessel.

The tactics inflicted heavy losses on American forces and "instilled terror on board ships," according to some historians.

"Few missiles or weapons have ever spread such flaming terror, such torturing burns, such searing death, as did the kamikaze in his self-destroying onslaughts," wrote naval historian Samuel Eliot Morison.

Creston agrees. During one of the attacks, his brother became trapped.

"He was in a room for 20 hours. They had to cut him out with torches," Creston said.

His Last Battle

Creston, 68, says he respected his brother for going into the U.S. Navy in wartime. Still, he admits, he was saddened by his death. From time to time, he pulls out a video documentary on the battle that ended his brother's life.

The tape is called, "The Ship that Wouldn't Die." It reminds Creston of Elwood.

During his last battle, Elwood worked as a machine mate third class on the *Franklin*. He probably worked in the engine room, according to Creston.

The *Franklin* was the fifth war ship to be named for Benjamin Franklin. It stood about 15 stories high. Its length was the size of three football fields. Some called it "Big Ben."

At 7:08 a.m. on March 19, the carrier fell under attack by a Japanese dive bomber. It was between 50 and 60 miles off the coast of Japan. For several hours, ammunition exploded. Supplies burned. Gasoline poured from the side of the *Franklin* like a flaming Niagara.

"It's amazing that anybody survived it," says Creston. "There were so many bodies, so badly burned. My brother either burned to death or suffocated."

A Chaplain Remembers

In addition to the thousands of sailors aboard the *Franklin*, Father Joseph T. O'Callahan also was present. He gives a chilling description of what happened in his book, *I Was Chaplain on the Franklin*. He said the whole ship quivered in a mighty blast.

Creston Bumbaugh holds a picture of his brother Elwood, who was killed on the USS *Franklin*.

"As in a great storm," he wrote, "disaster struck with a wild wind. But this wind was flame, burning gasoline. Starting at the hangar deck, it burst forward with hurricane speed. One breath of that wind could sear a man's lungs.

"The hurricane raced on, leaving the hangar deck heaped with corpses. It shriveled planes in its path, while each plane gave new impetus to the storm—300 gallons of new impetus—and there were 40 planes parked on the hangar deck."

The chaplain said that as they passed Indian-filed behind the elevator bulkhead, the open pit, a few inches of steel away, was like a corked retort full of burning gases. Explosive pressure was trapped between the side bulkheads and the heavy elevator locked into the flight deck.

"Something had to give," he said.

"A massive blast shook the entire ship," he continued. "With a mighty smash the elevator was torn from its locks and pushed eight or 10 feet upward. The succeeding vacuum sucked it back, and it fell into the pit. We lost our footing, and we nearly lost our lives. Why hadn't the light bulkhead given way instead of the heavy elevator? At the time we didn't realize how close death had come."

As for Elwood, Creston did not learn about his death until April 5 of that year.

"I was 17 and working on the farm when I heard the news. I can take you right to the spot where I heard it," he says.

"I couldn't believe it. We'd been reading in the papers that the war was winding down. We were all surprised," he said.

"Oh, we were all hurt when we found out," he said.

An Inspiration

Despite the pain brought on by the loss, Creston would find inspiration through his brother and go on to join the military. He was drafted into the U.S. Army during the Korean War.

Like his brother, he also fell in love with the guitar and has played for years with his brother in mind. Creston and his wife Leona, along with their son Jonathan and daughter Sharon have made music a vital part of their family.

In speaking about his brother, Creston is careful to mention the others who died with him, such as William Frederick Chrisman, whose father once served as principal of Washington Township High School.

"They did what they had to do," he said.

10

DANIEL S. GEISER, JR.

Note: Much of the material in the story is based on an article by historian Nancy Bondurant Jones which appeared in the Daily News-Record. It is used with permission.

HARRISONBURG—The date was October 29, 1944. Daniel S. Geiser Jr. was aboard the USS *Iowa* near Manila Bay in the Philippines when he and his shipmate Ace Riggins volunteered to rescue two men in dangerous waters.

The two men were downed aviators, floating in a life raft about 150 miles away.

"On leaving the Iowa, we were told enemy aircraft were in the vicinity and therefore the task force would begin highspeed retirement when the last planes were recovered at dusk," recalled Geiser, who was serving as a pilot in the U.S. Naval Reserve.

"We were warned again that Rats and Hawks, Japanese aircraft, had been sighted," Geiser said. "With F6F's (Hellcats) flying high cover, we headed east."

Geiser and Riggins both knew that the distance meant the rescue would take most of the daylight hours. Neither one of them wanted to make a night landing. The reason was simple: Such landings were extremely tough and hard to make.

Despite the fear and the dangers involved, however, Geiser pulled it off. The rescue ran as planned, "though the sea was choppy," he said.

While putting his own life at risk, he bravely helped the two downed fliers aboard and took off to join Riggins and the Hellcats in the air.

The Medal

Shortly after the incident, Geiser was presented the Distinguished Flying Cross. The script that accompanied the medal said he received the honor "for heroism and extraordinary achievement in aerial flight as pilot of a Scout Observation Seaplane, attached to the USS *Iowa*, during operations in enemy Japanese-controlled waters of the Pacific, on October 29, 1944.

"Courageously volunteering to undertake the rescue of two pilots forced down in the vicinity of the Philippines, Lt. Geiser skillfully flew his plane to the designated area approximately 150 miles distant and, despite extremely adverse conditions, picked up the two survivors and effected a successful takeoff with the overloaded plane."

Today, Geiser, a native of Waynesboro, Pennsylvania, lives with his wife Betty, in Harrisonburg, Virginia. He taught at Bridgewater College and directed athletics for 20 years (1946 to 1966). Later, he taught at American University until his retirement in 1983, the year he returned to Harrisonburg.

Although much has happened over the last 50 years, Geiser can still see the flames from Japanese firing. He can still see the smoke from deadly explosions. The smell of sea water remains fresh in his nostrils. He remembers the fears and the feats of brave men pitted against the enemies of nature, as in stormy waters, as well as the enemies of the flesh, as in Japanese.

Geiser's Aircraft

Geiser made the daring rescue in a plane which was designed, primarily, for observation and scouting, and some rescues. He flew a late model Kingfisher of the OS2U series. It was powered by a 450-horsepower Pratt & Whitney engine.

The Kingfisher had a fixed Browning .30-caliber machine gun in its nose and a flexible .30-caliber machine gun in the rear cockpit. Although the Kingfisher OS2U was not designed for hot battles, it is believed to be the first monoplane to serve aboard battleships.

According to Geiser, battleships and cruisers carried planes and catapulted them off into the air at 70 mph, or enough to become airborne.

"For (the plane's) return, the ships made a 90-degree turn though wind to create smooth water for landing," Geiser said. "Planes taxied up to the stern and were lifted back to the catapult by crane."

Some pilots who landed on flight decks felt it was a "tougher assignment," Geiser said.

Geiser describes a typical mission of the Kingfisher:

"Heavy guns on ships shot over the horizon, dropped their shells and couldn't see the target visually. So they put these planes up over the target to call the fall of shot and radio back."

Lest one should think these planes as mere weaklings during the war, one need only recall a couple of historic rescues made by the Kingfisher. One that stands out occurred almost two years before Geiser's rescue. It happened on November 11, 1942, when a Kingfisher rescued four men who had been adrift for three weeks.

"One of those rescued was World War I ace Eddie Rickenbacker," writes historian Nancy Bondurant Jones. "Unable to pull all the men into the aircraft, the pilot lashed Rickenbacker and another man to the wing and then taxied about 40 miles to land."

Another notable rescue occurred on April 30, 1944, in Truk Lagoon, were 22 men were saved in one day by two Kingfishers and the submarine USS *Tang*, noted Jones. One photo shows the Kingfisher taxiing to the sub with eight airmen on its wings and fuselage, she said.

Unwelcome Surprises

Geiser knew his mission in October of 1944. He knew the risks. But despite his training—and the fact that he had picked up the downed aviators—a few surprises awaited him.

After he picked up the two survivors and joined Riggins and the Hellcats in the air, a heavy line squall formed between the planes. That, plus darkness and an impending gasoline shortage, forced Geiser down.

"We decided to land and wait out the storm on the water," he said. "Hearing this, Bingo 40 (one of the Hellcats) said he would land near us and we could bring him aboard.

"I landed in a rough sea away from the storm and saw Riggins land a short distance away. Bingo 40 came low overhead and crash landed not very far off the port quarter."

Geiser saw Riggins for the last time as he began to taxi toward the downed Bingo 40.

"I was doing all I could to keep the plane afloat while searching the area without success," he said.

Jones, who interviewed Geiser at length, said that while the rescued pilots may have been cramped in their close quarters, their extra weight may have been instrumental in keeping the Kingfisher afloat. Geiser used the engine to keep the plane headed into the wind until the storm subsided, she wrote, adding that fear and despondency started to creep in.

Realizing the task force had planned high-speed retirement at dusk, the three men felt there would be little concern for their "small group as compared to the concern for the safety of thousands," remembers Geiser. With that in mind, the men stood nervously on the wing and watched ever so carefully for help, should they be so lucky. While standing on the wing, they spotted blinking lights moving fast in their direction.

"Who is it?" they wondered, believing it to be a Japanese ship.

"They couldn't be American ships because of the darkened-ship policies and strict restrictions on showing a light at night," Geiser said. "Hours had gone by since friendly ships left the area."

A Desperate Ploy

After a while the men put their heads together and devised a plan. They agreed on a desperate ploy...something they hoped would complete their rescue and keep them alive.

"Sure the OS2U would be followed by the Japanese," said Geiser, "so we jumped into the water holding on to a two-man life raft and hoped to be overlooked."

That plan did not work.

"A ship hull appeared beside us. We heard some English words from the deck, spoken by Japanese, we thought," said Geiser.

They were wrong.

They climbed aboard the destroyer USS *Colohan*, and Geiser was taken back to the *Iowa*. Once on board, writes Jones, "he was relieved to see a plane secure in the catapult, certain that Riggins had made it. He soon discovered it was his own plane."

A number of planes were downed because of the storm. Therefore, the entire Task Force remained to search for and pick up pilots.

"They had my plane on radar," said Geiser. "Around 4 a.m., when they sighted the now-empty, moving Kingfisher, the ship drew alongside and the first lieutenant, using a megaphone, yelled at the moving aircraft, telling the pilot to wake up."

At that point, the *Iowa* made a 360-degree turn and again came beside the now stationary, out-of-fuel Kingfisher.

"The Iowa stopped dead in the water, backed down, and lowered a crewman by the stern crane to attach the hook and hoisted the crewman and plane back to the catapult," Geiser said.

He was then told to report to the bridge, where he was lauded for a job well done.

"To this day," said Geiser, "I can't figure the expression on Captain McCann's face. Was it a hint of a smile...when I gave my reason for leaving the Kingfisher?

"Did he expect me to know that there were no enemy ships in the area?"

PART 4

HOPING AGAINST HOPE

Keeping Faith as a Prisoner of War

Dwight F. Hastings during the war.

11

Dwight F. Hastings

WAYNESBORO—Moments after releasing his chute, Dwight F. Hastings landed in a freshly cleared wheat field. A bit dazed from the impact, he looked up and saw a German farmer waving a pitchfork at him. He looked around and saw another man; this one had a rifle and was running toward him.

Hastings, 23 at the time, braced himself for the worst. Still, he was caught off guard.

"I looked around and saw a long rifle being pointed between my eyes from a distance of three or four feet," remembers Hastings, who is now 73. "I thought my time had about arrived as I stared at the man with the rifle."

That was the beginning of Hastings' life as a prisoner of war in Germany. He had fallen after his plane was hit. He would go on to experience life as he never knew it.

Before the Military

Hastings was a tall, lanky kid before entering the military. In 1939, he graduated from Bethesda Chevy Chase High School while the country was still struggling through the depression. In November of that year, he began working as a machinist apprentice at Landis Tool Company in Waynesboro.

After he completed his trade in 1942, the war caught his attention. One by one, each of his friends from high school—and his place of work—started signing up for the military. At that time, the yearning to join became an itch for him. It was something he had to scratch.

"I, too, felt compelled to try and get into the Army Air Corps for pilots," he said form his massive home on Woodlea Drive. "So without telling the company what I was doing, I went to Harrisburg in August 1942 and took the entrance exams to get in, and was sort of surprised at how many of the others doing this were college graduates."

Hastings passed all the tests and signed up. He later told the company of his decision and found a disappointing reaction.

"They acted hurt because they said they were going to get me deferred from the draft as they needed the expertise I had acquired while working there for the war effort."

Hastings, however, felt the company had been playing favorites by deferring those with family connections to the company, "while allowing some of the best machinists to be drafted, and told them I just felt compelled to go."

After Hastings passed his tests and was given the go-ahead to join the Air Force, he had to wait until February before being called to active duty. During that wait, he experienced more than the anxiety many felt before entering the service. He also experienced romance.

"While I was awaiting the call to active duty, I met My Jeanie on a blind date arranged by mutual friends and we fell hard!" he says with a laugh.

Even though she had lived only a block and a half from where he roomed, he did not see her until after he signed up for the military. After meeting her, he fell in love and became engaged.

But duty was calling and he reported on February 27, 1943.

"The waiting from August until February was made endurable by providing me more time for courting Jeanie."

After his training, Hastings would fly in 43 combat missions. His last one occurred on August 7, 1944.

The Frightening Hole

The morning of August 7, 1944, Hastings briefed his crew and boarded the B-17G aircraft.

"I remember Sergeant Howard Kidney, the ball turret gunner, telling me that he was certainly going to walk out of Germany if we were shot down because he believed his wife was expecting to have their first child momentarily," Hastings said.

Kidney had a pair of GI boots and his 45 pistol.

"I reminded him of the strong recommendation of our company commander to not take hand guns on missions because of evidence that captured airmen who did so were sometimes killed by their own guns."

That day, however, Hastings said his close friend—and bunk mate—Dominic Siani had arranged to fly with his crew as bombardier on what was to be his 50th—and last—mission.

For a while, things were going smoothly. Hastings and his crew were leading the No. 4 squadron on the Blechhammer, Silesia, bombing mission to the target area.

"As the No. 4 squadron leader, our position within the six squadron formation of the 2nd Bomb Group placed us right in the middle of the group as viewed from the ground," Hastings said.

He said they heard all five of the 88 anti-aircraft shell bursts (they were fired in clips of five shells) which rocked the plane as they were on the bomb run.

"Right after 'bombs away' we were trying to evaluate our damage as smoke was being reported by crew members in the rear of the aircraft. When I looked back along the trailing edge of the left wing, I saw a frightening hole fairly close to the fuselage with what looked like a very large blow torch-like flame reaching back several feet."

Hastings quickly ordered the crew to bail out. He dumped the stick forward to try to pick up speed. He wanted to move out of the formation and "try and drag the fire back to delay any explosion as long as possible."

He was not lucky.

Desperately, he tried to set the automatic pilot so he and the crew could all get out with little trouble. That didn't work. It had been shot out. So he then trimmed the controls as best he could in an attempt to keep it in a dive while he escaped.

"The crew responded to my order to bail out with remarkable haste," he said. "When I felt I was ready to go, I looked back to find my good friend Dominic Siani looking up through the hatch to see how I was doing.

"I motioned for him to go out, and swung down to go myself. As I left my seat I noticed no movement anywhere within the plane, and with all doors open I could see it was empty."

Soon after the chute opened, Hastings saw the plane going away.

"I was rocked around by what must have been the concussion from the plane exploding for I then discovered there was a hole in the chute, probably made by shrapnel from the plane. I hoped it would not get any bigger."

Another concern was that a German fighter plane, possibly a Me-09, was swinging toward him in a way that could lead to strafing him, but then the German kept turning and Hastings saw that he was on fire and slowly spiraling toward the ground.

On landing, Hastings found himself surrounded by angry Germans. They were armed with forks and rifles. When Hastings found a rifle pointed between his eyes, an SS Captain appeared and kicked the rifle out of the man's hands. He confiscated the weapon and kicked the man away from the group.

"I obviously was to be his prisoner, and recognized as being an officer, I was to be taken alive."

The Germans ripped off all of Hastings' clothes and searched him for weapons. They allowed him then to put his clothes back on and put him in the back seat of a Ford with a first lieutenant.

While Hastings and the Germans were riding, the lieutenant tried to compliment him through broken English. He said he admired Hastings because of the way he responded—he kept his cool—and did not flinch when the rifle was pointed at him. Curious, he asked Hastings whether he had been a Boy Scout in America. Hastings confirmed it. The lieutenant then said he, too, had been one.

A Warm Memory

After a short distance, the Ford broke down in a village. Immediately, people and soldiers surrounded the car, yelling,

"Amerikanisches Schwein" and Amerikanischer Gangster." Many shook pitchforks and their fists at Hastings.

"The veins stood out in their foreheads—convincing me that there were very strong feelings being expressed, and that it was to my advantage to have been picked by the SS Captain and his men.

"A couple of the enlisted men were working feverishly on the engine for what seemed like a very long time to me, and the demonstration continued. I then had a strange experience. I noticed that a woman about my mother's age was smiling, and then I realized that I was smiling also, and something about this woman's actions seemed to change the whole tone of the crowd.

"I didn't hear the "Gangster" and "Schwein" words anymore. The engine started, and we went on to what may have been the next town where I was relegated to a chair in the center portion of what was probably a town hall meeting room.

Hastings said he will never forget that moment.

After waiting for more than an hour, Hastings heard a commotion. He looked around and saw Dominic Siani, his friend and bombardier, who had landed about two miles on the opposite side of the town and had been forced to walk with a gun in his back—on a sprained or broken ankle—all the way to this town hall.

"He was ghostly white and in obvious pain, but it was good to find each other, even though they didn't want us to talk to each other."

Hastings and Dom were later taken to a German Air Force transport which took them to a Luftwaffe Base. At the base they were put into separate cells for the night. That evening, the Germans brought Hastings a large bowl of boiled potatoes with skins on, "and I ate the whole thing, much to the amazement of my handlers. I later learned that the Germans didn't eat potato skins because of the German practice at that time of using human manure as fertilizer."

The men also were taken to Dulag Luft, the Luftwaffe Interrogation Center outside Frankfurt where they were questioned relentlessly.

"Our food fare in solitary was ersatz coffee and a piece of dark bread in the morning, a very weak potato soup with a piece of dark bread with a little ersatz jam at noon, and a repeat of the noon meal in the evening."

Dwight F. Hastings in 1995.

Hastings was permitted to go down the hall to the bathroom once in the morning and once at night. Even that, he remembers, was not an automatic allowance as he had to ask for it each time.

As Hastings tried to adjust to these strange experiences, he struggled to sleep in the bed which was made of a wooden frame with about five slats holding a flat straw-stuffed mattress bag. The bag was thin, hard and uncomfortable.

"I remember buttoning the collar of my shirt tight at the neck to try and keep as warm as possible at night, because there was generally no heat in the room."

Hastings also discovered fleas in the room that caused the inside of the collar to be spotted with red from the bites.

Hastings spent 12 days in solitary confinement at Dulag Luft. During that time, he said the food did not get any better. To pass the time, he would tap Morse code messages to a young English enlisted airman he saw at the door next to his as he received his soup ration.

The enlisted man seemed frightened. "He immediately responded and we chatted in this time-consuming way over several days."

Following his stay in confinement, Hastings was shipped out to a prison camp in Stalag Luft III. On his arrival, other American prisoners interrogated him to make sure he was not a German infiltrator. The whole atmosphere in the camp was run in a military fashion with the senior American officer in charge.

Hastings was assigned to a room with 12 bunks (four triple decker bunks) in wooden barracks.

"Our day-to-day existence was limited. We were always hungry. The food allotments diminished as the war dragged on."

Although Hastings and the other prisoners were short on food for the body, they had plenty for the mind. Because the camp was so well established, book parcels had been accumulated and consolidated for us by all "Kriegies" in a library near the barracks.

"I believe I read about 35 books in the five months before the evacuation of Stalag Luft III on the night of January 27, 1945. About 2,000 officers in our ...camp (mostly college educated), representing all sorts of diversified talents, set up courses for study, amateur theatrical productions and improvised stage performances and many surprising activities I hadn't expected to find in a POW camp."

Other Worries

When the Americans were not reading books, they were reading letters from home. Many of them received "Dear John" letters which told of girlfriends or fiancees who could not wait for them. Back home, the women either married other men or simply lost interest because of the long absence.

"One (American) started a collection of pictures of the errant girlfriends and wives, and I believe he had collected about 25 when I talked with him. One fellow worried about his wife's letters telling him of the wonderful times she was having at some resort with her girlfriend, two wonderful guys—and his allotment check she was getting. This man turned totally gray in a very short time."

The Liberation

A day before Hastings' camp was liberated by the 14th Armored Division (under General George Patton), he and the American prisoners got word that help was coming.

"And we were told the Germans were going to fight for the camp. Early the next day we saw a bunch of German soldiers assembling in a field next to our camp, and we got the idea they were more apt to be getting ready to surrender than to fight.

"Then after they had disappeared, we heard rifle fire. It was interesting to find many of the airmen in the camp were standing out by the fence trying to see what was going on, while officers who had seen some action on the ground were flat under a bunk, or making as low a profile as possible."

Hastings heard later that a German officer had approached the gate from the outside with orders that the German authorities in charge of the camp were to fight to the last man.

"I understood that only one 14th Armored Division soldier was lost in the battle for Moosburg, but a large number of Germans were killed. Only one 'Kriegie' was hit by a stray bullet, and he was not critically wounded."

April 29, 1945 was a special day for Hastings. On that day he saw an American tank.

"It was a very emotional experience to see our first American tank drive through the front gate. We swarmed all over it. We had all forgotten what healthy, mature American men looked like.

"I had never seen such a fine looking bunch of men as those representing the 14th Armored Division. A day or two later Patton came strolling into the camp on an inspection visit. He had just been made a three star general."

Hastings said Patton advertised his promotion with many three star insignias—all over the place.

"His pearl handled pistols (on each hip) looked to be recently polished. I was impressed by the vigor and size of the man. He walked around most our camp, but the colonel and aides accompanying him all had to trot and then walk and trot some more just to keep up with him. His visit was a great morale boost."

PART 5

CLOSE CALLS

A Combat Engineer Discovers the Power of Prayer

Fred Rock in 1995.

12

Fred J. Rock

FAYETTEVILLE—All battles were bad, but some were much worse than others, according to Fred J. Rock, who served with the 27th Combat Engineers in the war.

He said the fact that some were worse than others can be seen in the battles he had in New Guinea and Leyte Gulf, where many a man died on the field.

"Those were hard times," he says.

In New Guinea, Rock's mission was to land and fill up a position to hold back the Japanese. He was 21 at the time.

"We dug in with the Infantry. We worked with them. But we had the flame throwers to burn the Japs out who had dug in."

Although Rock's mission was clear, he said the Japanese were well placed in New Guinea, and that they had some pretty good snipers. Snipers who triggered fear in American soldiers.

"A lot of things shake you up, especially losing a friend," he said. The only thing worse than that is the thought of losing your own life, he said, adding he had a number of close calls.

Close Call in New Guinea

One such close call occurred in New Guinea.

"The Japs always attacked at night. We'd push in the daytime."

Rock had to take some supplies and machine guns with barbed wire and ammunition to troops up front.

"We were told the Japs had broken through and our men needed help."

Because the Americans moved during the day, Rock and a comrade took a truck and commenced to travel to the front lines. They started up and began moving with caution. They were fully aware of their environment. They knew the enemy could surprise them at any moment in the thick jungles of New Guinea.

When the truck reached about six miles from its destination, a sniper fired. Rock started praying. He and his friend wondered if they would ever deliver the supplies. Although they had only six miles to go, Rock said that as the snipers started firing, those six miles became the longest six miles of his life.

"You never knew if you were going to make it. But we did."

Rock felt good about delivering the supplies. The mission, however, was not over, as he and his friend had to turn back.

They first tried to take the route they had used earlier, but came under Japanese fire.

"We made our own road. We knocked down stuff you never seen to reach the beach. We thought we had made it."

Close to the shore, Rock and his friend encountered nine Japanese who were guarding the beach with three machine guns.

A Long Night

"They were shooting at us, so my friend and I jumped out of the truck and into the sand. We started pushing it up to form a wall—so they couldn't hit us."

They lay there in the sand through the early part of the night. After a while, the friend thought they should make a break for the ocean. That was around 1 a.m.

"The water was about 100 yards away. He thought it was the only way to survive. I didn't think it was a good idea."

The two men argued about the decision.

"I told him we'd never make it with the moon shining so bright. Then he gave me 15 minutes to decide what to do."

Like the six miles earlier, the 15 minutes seemed longer than usual. Still, he thought about. He considered his options and prayed.

"I really prayed. My mother had been a Christian, and she brought me up in a Christian home. So I asked the Lord for help."

Moments later, Rock got the idea of holding up his helmet.

"I told him that before we move, I wanted to try something. I took my helmet off and put it on my gun. I then laid down on my back with the helmet up about three feet."

The second it appeared, Rock saw a flash of fire.

"At least 30 bullets from a machine gun ripped the helmet apart. My friend saw that and said, 'I'm glad I listened to you.'"

Rock then told him, "If we're going to get out of here alive, somebody will have to get us out."

The Rescue

Fortunately, American soldiers were moving in.

Every three hours, Rock would hold up his helmet. Each time he did, the Japanese would fire.

"A patrol heard the gun fire and moved in our direction. By 1 p.m. a squad began firing. I could tell they were Americans."

Rock said, you don't know what it is like to hear your people in those circumstances.

Tearfully, he said, "When you're cut off and you're run down and scared to death, words can't describe what you feel when you hear Americans talking."

Close Call in Leyte Gulf

Rock had other close calls. Once while taking Leyte Gulf, he and his men faced the dreaded Kamikazes and Japanese fire from the skies. "The Japanese had lots of air and they wanted to kill as many Americans as possible."

On one occasion, he and a friend hit the beach running as the enemy fire missed them by inches. Quickly, to escape the fire, they tried to hide behind the big wheels of a truck.

Rock dove first. His friend followed. The planes kept firing.

When Rock pushed his friend to ask a question, he did not move. Rock turned and found him bleeding. He'd been hit while diving behind the wheels.

"He was alive then, but I don't know whether he lived."

Rock is extremely grateful that he made it home after the war. He says he has no regrets.

"You felt what you were doing was the right thing," he said. "You have to have faith in the Lord. I've seen a lot of boys crack under the pressure. I mean crack up!"

"They couldn't take it. But I don't know what I would have done without the Lord."

PART 6

FINAL MOMENTS

The Bombing of Japan

David S. Brown during the war.

13

David S. Brown

As a 28-year-old in 1945, David S. Brown played a major role in bringing World War II to an end: He helped assemble the bombs that struck Hiroshima and Nagasaki—and made Japan surrender.

Because he had been in the military since September 1940, Brown, who lives with his wife, Estelle, at 12615 Old Germantown Road, said he was tired of fighting and the Japanese just wouldn't quit. The bombs were the only thing that got their attention, he said.

"I was war-weary already," Brown said from his home. "I was ready for anything that could put an end to it."

The atom bomb dropped on Hiroshima in 1945 killed about 100,000 people. The one dropped on Nagasaki three days later killed another 40,000.

Thousands more who escaped immediate injury died in the years which followed because of the exposure to the radiation released by the bomb's explosion.

Secret Assignments

Brown, 78, admits the subject is a sensitive one for many people today, especially the Japanese. Still, he said, it was something that had to be done.

He remembers the events which led to his role in assembling the bombs.

On May 19, 1945, he was assigned to the 216th Army Air Force Base in Wendover, Utah.

"The security was so tight in that unit. We were not even allowed to discuss anything," he said.

On May 27, he was assigned to the 1st Ordnance Squadron Aviation of the 509th Composite Group, the corps of men who assembled and dropped the bomb.

At that time, Brown, a first lieutenant, worked as an ordinance officer.

"We knew we were being assigned to a special unit, but we did not know what or where," he said. "We were under strict orders not to talk to anyone."

The Big Question

Soon after joining the secretive and elite group, a stranger who was neatly dressed and very formal approached Brown. He asked him a question that Brown said he will never forget.

"How would you like to be associated with a project that could mean the end of this war immediately and possibly the end of all wars?"

The man, a security officer, told Brown to think about it. He did not want an immediate answer.

"Twenty-four hours later, he questioned us again," Brown said, adding that while he was for it, he "had no idea of the magnitude of the project."

On June 15, Brown's birthday, the crew boarded the USS *Corvus* and set sail for Saipan and Tinian, two islands near Guam.

While on Tinian, Brown worked as a utility maintenance officer. He and his men prepared to set up for the bomb.

"We were isolated from the rest of the Air Force people. Security was so tight, we were virtually prisoners," he said.

The job was not only highly secretive, it was scary.

"We built the bombs without benefit of drawings or written instructions. It was done by word-of-mouth instructions."

David S. Brown in 1995.

At the start of the project, Brown heard news which could be called dreadful.

"We knew what we were trying to do, but they told us that if it didn't work, no one would know what happened to us. We would disappear from the face of the earth," he said.

The news, however, did not scare young Brown.

"I guess I was fatalistic," he said. "We realized war had its risks."

Following a test fire in New Mexico, Brown said they knew the bombs would work.

At 2 a.m., August 6, they loaded the first bomb called "Little Boy," on a B-29 bomber nicknamed the "Enola Gay." The bomb weighed about 9,000 pounds.

"I remember it. We loaded her and she took off. I was sitting at the end of the runway with a chaplain as she took off," Brown said.

About 8:30 that morning, Brown learned it had been dropped.

"We waited for an evaluation of the mission," he said. "Two days later we learned there was nothing left standing."

The Report

In addition to receiving the news by word of mouth, Brown's unit read about the news in a brief bulletin called "Daily Mission," provided by the 313th Bombardment Wing. Dated August 8, it carried the blaring headline: "Atomic Fury Hits Japan, Japs Acknowledge Hiroshima Blast."

An excerpt from the bulletin reads:

"The United States unleashed the most terrible weapon in history—an atomic bomb carrying the destructive power of 20,000 tons of TNT.

"President Truman made the initial announcement that the U.S. and British scientists had won the race to unlock the power of the atom, saying the 1st atomic bomb had been dropped on the city of Hiroshima 16 hours before.

"One bomb alone carries more wallop than 2,000 B-29s carrying high explosives. . .the power of the bomb was such as to stagger the imagination and would prove a tremendous aid in shortening the war.

"President Truman said the surrender ultimatum had been issued in an effort to spare the Jap people from utter destruction. 'Now,' he said, 'they can expect a rain of ruin the like of which has never been seen on this earth. . .

'We are now prepared to obliterate completely every productive enterprise the Japs have above ground in any city. Let there be no mistake we shall completely destroy Japan's power to make war.' "

Tough Decision

The decision to use the atomic bomb was a tough one, Brown said, and one he admires Truman for making.

"I personally believe it was a proper one and it did save an untold number of lives," he said. "Japanese mentality at the time was to die in service of the emperor. They would have fought to the death."

Brown said they had hoped Japan would "see the light" after the first bomb.

"Then word came down to go with the second one, called 'Fat Man.' That was the one that really triggered the proceedings for Japan's surrender," he said.

But what of the deaths of the civilians?

"You always have misgivings about civilians," Brown said, "but war knows no sex, age or whatever. War is a terrible thing."

In short, Brown said his view of the bombing is similar to that of Chuck Sweeney, a pilot who flew on both bombing missions.

"Our overriding desire was to shorten the war. I'd seen too many 22-year-olds come back whitehaired from the terror of amphibious landings," Sweeney said.

Author's Note

When I think of the creation of this book and the events that brought it together, I can only say that life is full of surprises. For what began as a tiny stream of military interest, soon ended in an ocean of oral history and a loving devotion to World War II veterans.

The experience of doing research, interviewing veterans and their loved ones, hearing their stories and struggling to tell them without exaggeration, but with conviction and authority, turned out to be more than a blessing. In no uncertain terms, the whole experience was educational. It was captivating, at times, hypnotizing, and yes, intoxicating. In other words, I enjoyed everything about the process and feel I'm a better person because of it.

Although the experience has been enlightening and a lot of fun, I do not mean to suggest it was easy. Why?

It was not. In fact, it proved to be challenging. And it was so for at least three reasons.

The First Reason

First, it was challenging for emotional reasons on the part of the veterans. Many found it extremely difficult to talk about the war. They could not do it without having an onslaught of deep emotions mingled with tears.

Even though their experiences happened 50 years ago, they could recall numerous details, as if the war was only yesterday. Still, despite the pain, the men often broke down and shared their stories anyway. Muscling through a wall of reluctance, they managed to relive some of the most horrible moments in history.

Many said that when they spoke with me, it was the first time they ever talked about the war. As the stories appeared in print, children of the vets were both shocked and proud. "I didn't know," their children said. "I never knew Dad experienced all that."

For the most part, the interviews reminded me of a statement by Studs Terkel. He said that in recalling an epoch, some of his subjects "experienced pain, in some instances; exhilaration, in others. Often it was a fusing of both. A hesitancy, at first, was followed by a flow of memories: long-ago hurts and small triumphs. Honors and humiliations. There was laughter, too."

The Second Reason

The second reason this project was challenging was because of the emotions I felt as a writer. Not a few times, I wept during the interviews. Other times, I wept as I drove home or while I was writing the stories.

There were times when I would lay awake at night tossing and turning as I pondered the lead (the opening paragraph) and format for the stories. You see, these stories were not just stories to me. They were not just "features." They were astounding moments recaptured. They were history brought to life, precious and hidden memories unveiled. In short, the stories to me, were heartwarming and gut-wrenching. They spoke of faith and fear. Tears and laughter. The stories were about life and death and the people who knew both.

In all honesty, the vivid manner in which the men talked about the war had a powerful impact on my own thoughts, my views and my imagination. At times, I felt myself being transported through the freezing cold of the Battle of the Bulge. I could feel the snow which was knee-deep and see the blood of American soldiers. Through the veterans, I could hear the cries of dying marines on Iwo Jima. I could hear the Japanese kamikazes in the waters of the Pacific, and see the flames aboard U.S. carriers.

The Third Reason

The third reason this project proved challenging was because of the nature of writing. It was hard work, anyway you cut it, anyway you look at it.

For me, writing has always been tough and it never comes easy. I suppose I can identify with William Zinsser, who said, "writing wasn't easy and it wasn't fun. It was hard and lonely, and the words seldom just flowed."

My respect for writing and the wisdom of Zinsser reached a new height as I labored on this book.

"Writing is hard work," he wrote. "A clear sentence is no accident. Very few sentences come out right the first, or even the third time....If you find that writing is hard, it's because it is hard. It's one of the hardest things that people do."

I can only say that I agree. Like Ernest Hemingway, I tried hard "to get it right." And that took a lot of time, effort and sweat. The stories are not perfect and were not meant to be. But they are my best at what I could do under the circumstances in which they were written.

I must add, too, that my goal in writing these stories was not to imitate other writers nor to trivialize an experience through sensationalism. Instead, I wanted to tell the stories accurately, precisely and succinctly. My goal was to "tell it like it is" without editorial comment or prejudicial prodding.

History Brought to Life

The men in this book, through their sincerity, have brought history to life. For the first time in my own life, history was more than pages in a book. For the first time, it was taken out of the world of academia and the world of ivory towers. For the first time, history was made real and concrete. It was not just the footage of a documentary on late-night TV.

For the first time in my life, I began to understand World War II and the men who fought in that war.

Hence, I salute these men who helped to preserve the freedom we now enjoy in this nation and those abroad. Without a doubt, we are fortunate to have these men in our midst today.

It is my hope that we talk with them. Learn from them. Record their stories and preserve them for generations to come.

As I bring this to a close, I ask that we remember a statement by Ronald Reagan.

"As you look toward the future, always remember the treasures of our past," he said. "Every generation stands on the shoulders of the generation that came before. Jealously guard the values and principles of our heritage. They did not come easy."

Roscoe Barnes III
September 1995

ACKNOWLEDGMENTS

I have had the good fortune to have the support of many people who have generously put their experience, their patience, their concern and their expertise at my disposal. In all honesty, this book would not have been born without their direct or indirect contributions.

Because it is easy to inadvertently omit someone when gratitude is expressed, some people refuse to mention any names at all, for fear of offending some generous person. That concern is understandable. It also is a concern of mine. Still, however, I'm going to be daring. I'm going to make an attempt to name the people who played such an important role in the writing and publication of this book.

Should I fail to mention someone who deserves credit, I will say now that the omission was unintentional and that I am sorry. To that person, I can only say the input was deeply appreciated.

The first person I must thank is Sue Ernde, the editor of *The Record Herald.* These stories were written under her direction and because of her suggestions. The second person I must thank is Kelly Luvison, the publisher of *The Record Herald.* He put his stamp of approval on the stories and gave permission for their use in book form.

Next, I want to thank Harold Collier, the publisher of White Mane Publishing Company, for his interest and faith in this work. I'm grateful to him and his entire staff. Vicki Stouffer and Denise Dennis, two staff members of White Mane, were very patient and extremely helpful in getting this book off the ground.

Annette Dorty and Sid Miller also were helpful. Annette worked relentlessly and skillfully in designing the contents of this book. Sid, a master photographer, was there to develop the photos.

I also want to thank Jean Walck, Amy Giancoli, Wanda Moebius, Lee Goodwin, Scott Weaver, Shawn Hardy, Don Aines, Jill Ercolino, Joyce F. Nowell and the rest of *The Record Herald* staff.

Senator Terry Punt and Mark Nesbitt deserve a hearty salute for their support, along with Debbie Sanders, who encouraged me from the beginning. People like Robert Rock, Pete Walters, and Bob Thomas among others, provided me with good story ideas. Their suggestions were more than worthwhile. Bill Adams, one of the veterans featured here, provided lots of help with doing research.

Representative Pat Fleagle also was supportive.

Particular thanks are due to Historian Nancy Bondurant Jones of Harrisonburg, Virginia. She, a talented biographer, deserves credit for permitting the use her story on Daniel S. Geiser Jr. The story first appeared in the *Daily News-Record* of Harrisonburg.

Dwight Hastings was most helpful in not only telling his story, but in writing it as well. He provided me with a brief autobiographical piece he had written and copied for his friends and relatives.

In addition to these names, I must thank the readers of *The Record Herald*. Their response to these articles was both positive and encouraging. I would like particularly to express my debt to the veterans who are featured in this work. They, along with their relatives and friends, gave of their time to share these stories. May their stories be a legacy that will lead, inspire and live forever.

About The Author

ROSCOE BARNES III, the author of DISCOVER YOUR TALENT AND FIND FULFILLMENT, is an award-winning writer, an accomplished artist, popular speaker and successful minister.

AS A WRITER, he has worked as a news reporter for both military and civilian newspapers. In 1985, after working for *The Enterprise-Tocsin*, the Mississippi Press Association awarded him the First Place Award for Best Investigative Reporting. Since 1982, Barnes has published articles, book reviews, news stories and features in inspirational, military and trade magazines. He has published fiction in literary magazines in the United States and in Germany.

AS AN ARTIST, Barnes has worked as an illustrator for *The Nashville Graphic*, an award-winning newspaper where he also provided editorial cartoons on local and national issues. His illustrations have also appeared in magazines and been commissioned by churches, businesses, individuals, military officials, and legal associations. He is the author of BIG BUCKS FROM LITTLE SKETCHES (currently used by International Correspondence Schools.)

AS A SPEAKER, Barnes is in demand. For several years he hosted radio programs in several states. For the University of Maryland, he served as a Guest Lecturer and Writing Consultant for a Creative Writing course. For the National Bible Institute, he taught courses in Systematic Theology. After a successful interdenominational preaching workshop in Germany, a U.S. Army Chaplain and Post Commander named a quarterly workshop in his honor: "Barnes' Notes on Preaching", is the official title.

AS A MINISTER, Barnes has pastored churches since the early age of 17. He also served for seven years as a Chaplain's Assistant in the U.S. Army.

Barnes, who has done graduate work with Boston University, holds a Master of Arts degree from the Lutheran Theological Seminary (Gettysburg, PA). He earned his B.S. and A.S. degrees (Cum Laude) from East Coast Bible College (Charlotte, NC). He is a graduate and member of the Christian Writers Guild (Hume, CA). Barnes is a native of Indianola, Mississippi.